Denied Love

By Apostle Clarence Kittrell

Denied Love
Copyright © 2021 Clarence Kittrell
All rights reserved. No part of this publication may be
reproduced or transmitted in any form or by any means without
the written permission of the publisher.
ISBN: 1735812458
ISBN-13: 978-1-7358124-5-8

Contributing Editor: or all services completed
by Imprint Productions, Inc.
Cover Design: or all services completed
by Imprint Productions, Inc.

Printed in the United States of America
Published by Imprint Productions, Inc.
First Edition 2021
10 9 8 7 6 5 4 3 2 1

CONTENTS

	Acknowledgments	i
1	The Beginning	1
2	The Journey	8
3	Life Changing	17
4	Everything New	29
5	Beginning A Journey	41
6	Coming Into Understanding	56
7	Walking In The Work	65
8	Following The Vision Of Jesus Christ	72
9	Understanding The Vision	80
10	26th Year	86
11	I Am	98
	About The Author	103

ACKNOWLEDGMENTS

I want to thank my Lord and Savior Jesus Christ who is the keeper of my life. I am so glad he chose me as a person no one paid attention to, one who experienced denied love, but He showed me His love. I also want to thank my beautiful wife and my children. Also, I want to thank my spiritual Brothers and Sisters in Christ. I want to thank Imprint Productions, Inc's entire team. Pastor Brunetta Nelson has been very instrumental in this project. I also want to thank "The Ministry of Love and Deliverance," and those who support the ministry. I love you all. God Bless You!

Chapter 1
The Beginning

A long time ago, there was a man named James and a woman named Martha. James was handsome and very active in sports; he was a boxer, he ran track, played football, and basketball. He was extremely athletic and popular. Martha was in love with James and pursued him, but he did not want to settle for Martha. He had plans to go pro and so many other options. James was popular as a player of sports and the ladies.

Martha was a good student. However, while going to school, Martha also continued waiting, pursuing, and following James. Finally, one day they were together after a game. Martha had recently graduated from high school. She had planned to attend college in the fall, but she soon found out she was pregnant. Having lived in a very small town, Martha was subject to her parent's tradition, which maintained that if someone became pregnant, the only right thing to do was to marry. James was very, very upset about that because it stopped all that he desired to do.

They became married, the unlikely pair, James and Martha. James was high-spirited, and Martha had low self-esteem. However, while they continued their life together, they decided to move away from the small town where they were living. They moved north to a town called Muncie, Indiana, where they lived with their aunt. As they continued their lives, James' uncle helped him find a job. He went on about his life as Martha grew in her pregnancy. One day the babe was born - a baby girl whom they named Crystal. Crystal, however, was stillborn and passed away.

Though James and Martha were devastated, they moved on with their lives. Change continued to work in their lives while Martha went to school to become a registered nurse. While Martha was attending school, she and James married. It was during this time that she began working in a hospital. With time (a year-and-a-half later), Martha became pregnant again. This time, everything went fine. They named their little girl Karen, affectionately calling her "KK" as a nickname.

As Karen grew, all of James' family was very fond of her - so much so that Martha became highly bothered by it. It seemed to her that people preferred to give the baby far more attention than they did her. James attempted to convince her that it was her imagination and that she should stop worrying about it. However, she knew that something was wrong, so they moved into their own place and began living as a family.

Martha and James continued to live and work. They hired a babysitter to care for Karen. Suddenly, as life would have it, something happened again. This "something" was going to change their lives. Martha was pregnant again and not really ready for this pregnancy. Neither was James, who was highly agitated because he had not planned to have another child so soon. However, Martha's aunt reminded him, "It takes two to tango," so James just dealt with it.

This pregnancy was very different. The one thing about the baby forming inside Martha was that she was very sick from the moment she found out she was pregnant. Martha had no idea what was going on with her. However, as the baby grew, she noticed that the activity of this baby was remarkable. This child would not be still. Even the doctors were astonished that this child moved so much inside of her.

Because Martha was going to school, she loved to read. For some reason, although she was going to school and was almost finished obtaining her degree, she enrolled in more classes. This time she took on Bible classes. While Martha would be reading the Bible, every time she looked up, James was with his friends at the bar. She was getting really, really upset about it. So, the only thing she knew how to do, is what her aunt told her to do, "pray."

So, one day Martha's aunt gave her a Bible, and Martha began reading. The baby that was on the inside of her just would not be still. She would always talk to him, but that baby just kept kicking, moving, and moving. One day she picked up her Bible; having no idea where to start, she started in the Book of Genesis. She noticed that the baby would always keep still every time she read as if he was sitting there listening. She could not understand why he was always still during that time. Martha ignored it and continued to read. She read all from Genesis through Exodus. Every time Martha paused reading, it was as if the baby would turn over. And then when she stopped reading, she laid down, went to sleep, and then she ate. She knew when the baby was hungry. It was as if the baby formed inside her was already born because of how he was inside her. When Martha went to the doctor to have a check-up, she told him about it. The doctor stated that it was really abnormal for a baby inside the womb of six or seven months to be this active and doing these things. He requested that Martha keep them posted on the activity of the baby.

Martha continued to read, but she noticed something. By the time she got to Deuteronomy, something was happening; she began having dreams. In her dreams, it seems as though she could see her baby. Martha had no idea what was happening; it was as if someone was telling her about him - about this babe that was on the inside of her or about what was to happen. Martha told James about it. James kind of laughed at her, saying, "Yeah, right." He went about his way, and Martha got a little upset with him because she felt he was not listening to her.

James would always play with their other baby, Karen. Martha was getting jealous because it was as if he was forgetting about her. As time went on, she was getting near her due date. And she kept telling James that He needed to stay around because she was getting closer and closer to having the baby. James replied, "Don't worry. I'll be there. I'll be there. Stop worrying me." "Let me go out and have fun with my friends." So Martha cried. She was distraught, and she prayed for him. Almost suddenly, it was as if the baby told her to pick up the Bible because he became very feisty. As she started talking to him and rubbing her stomach, she said, "Baby, it will be okay, baby, it will be okay." As Martha started reading to him, he was still again, and he started listening. By the time she got to the Book of

Revelation, he was kicking. She didn't understand what was going on with him because there was one time that he was really, really still, but when she got towards the end of Revelation, he was kicking. She said, "Why is he kicking my stomach so hard? I thought that reading would keep him still." She was at nine months, and she thought that she would have at least two or three more weeks, but he kept kicking. She had no idea, so she went to have something to eat and continued to read to him. One day as she was having something to eat, she was reading to him. When she got to the last chapter of the book of Revelation, all of a sudden, her water broke.

Chapter 2
The Journey

When her water broke, it got to be exciting. Suddenly Martha took her phone and called her aunt. She inquired of her, "Have you seen James?" Her aunt told her no. Martha was really quite upset, and her aunt asked her what was going on? "My water broke," Martha said. Her aunt replied, "Well if you can't do anything, call a cab." Martha was upset because they were in the midst of a snowstorm." Martha retorted, "The cab won't be able to get to me. Let me make a few phone calls to see if I can find James." Right at that moment, she found James. He rushed to the house, got her in the car, and they began to drive. Even though they were sliding all over the place, he was able to get behind a slow snowplow and follow it all the way to the hospital. He said to her, "Hold on! Hold on. Don't have that baby in my car." As Martha was looking at him, she said, "I'm about to have the baby. I can't help it." Martha was distraught because James was worried more about his car than he was about her having the baby. They made it to the hospital just in time. They rushed her into the delivery room. Seconds later, the baby was born!

There was something different about this baby. James did not like the baby because this baby was not of the same complexion as he. And he wasn't the same complexion as Karen. James even questioned if the baby was his. He asked Martha, "Is this mine?" "Of course it's yours! I can't even believe that you would even say anything like this to me," Martha said. Settled, James said, "okay." So, she named him James Jr.

Martha looked at her baby and said, "James Jr.," he looked at her, and she said to him, "You have cost me a lot of things. I don't know what your life is going to be like but understand Mommy will always be here for you." Martha could not imagine what this baby would experience - this baby that was born. Martha remained in the hospital for a few more days and then brought James Junior home. When they came home, they noticed one little thing. Karen did not like her little brother. Little Karen was not receiving the attention she was used to receiving. As a result, little Karen would hit her brother. Martha told her that it was not nice and that she must not hit her little brother. So, little Karen cried and ran to her father. And James put little Karen in his arms and told her, "Oh, you're not being neglected, you're being loved." Because she was still very young, she didn't understand. However, this did not stop her from becoming jealous of her brother getting into things. Karen started acting out because she wanted attention from everyone.

Martha noticed one thing different. James did not want to pick up the baby. In his mind, he still felt like something was wrong because the baby did not have the same complexion as he. "I'm not crazy. I know something is wrong," James Sr. said. But what James didn't understand was that Martha hadn't been with anyone else. Martha had taken off from work because Little James Jr. had given her so much grief during her pregnancy. However, Martha continued living through everything she was living through and doing the things she was doing. She would breastfeed the baby. Every time it was time to eat, he was always ready to eat. She said, "He has a strong appetite." The doctor told Martha that the baby needed more than just breast milk for substance. You need to give him more. So, they try to give him different types of formula. Every kind of formula they tried was unsuitable for him. He would always get sick. Martha wondered what was going on with her baby. The doctor said they had no idea. They tried every type of formula for him. But James couldn't digest any of them properly. The baby's doctor said, "Well, I guess we have to go back to old school methods. Do all the things that we had to do before new things came about." So, they gave James goat milk, and goat milk was accepted.

James continued to grow and be well. He loved the goat's milk. He loved to eat and drink. The one thing that changed in Martha's life was that Martha would open her Bible in the middle of the night when the baby would not stop crying. She remembered how feisty he was during her pregnancy and how when she would start to read, he would stop moving. The baby would just be still. As Martha would read, James Jr. stopped, and he looked at her as if he was in a class. Martha said, "wow!" By the time she was at the end of a chapter, the boy would fall asleep. The only time he would get fret was when he was hungry. But when she opened the Bible to read to him, he would be quiet.

Martha noticed James Sr. was getting closer to his daughter, but he still did not want anything to do with little James Jr. This continued to upset Martha because she felt that it just wasn't right. She talked with her aunt about it, and they both talked to James. But James ignored it. He responded, "I don't think that this child is mine."

Martha continued to move forward with life. She exclaimed, "It doesn't matter because I'm going to take care of this baby. This baby will have the greatest of love." Martha had no idea what she had just said. There was another thing about this baby. James Jr. always laughed in his sleep. "I don't understand why you keep laughing and moving," said Martha. Her aunt told her, "I think you should call your Mom." When Martha called her mom and asked her about it, her mother told her the reason the baby was laughing was that there were Angels around him. They were entertaining the baby? She said, "Honey, don't be upset by what this baby is doing. God has something special for him." Martha listened to her mother and said, "I have no idea why but when he's upset, I read him the Bible, and he becomes quiet. And by the time I get to the end of the book of the Bible, he trips off into sleep." Her mother replied, "You have no idea what's about to happen in your life. He's going to change many people's lives. Martha, I know that I wasn't able to give you things in your life, and I know that hurt you, but I did the best I could." Martha understood. She hung up the phone, and as soon as she saw that James Jr. was hungry, she fed him and continued to read him the Bible.

James Jr. grew stronger and stronger. Martha would say to him, "You're starting to get a little bigger; it's kind of hard to carry you around." Little James Jr. didn't crawl; he scooted. One day while he was in his baby bed, he pulled up on the bed and lifted himself. Martha looked over at James Junior and said, "Are you trying to walk? Are you trying to get up?" As she picked him up, he smiled at her. She said, "Are you trying to walk?" He Laughed. Martha told him it was time to read and he laughed again. As she started to read, she set him down in his chair, but for some reason, James Jr. didn't want any food. So, she just continued on and read to him. As she was reading, he was quiet, but she had to stop because the phone rang. James Jr. was hungry. She fed him while she was talking on the phone, and he began eating. When Martha got off the phone, James Jr. didn't seem to want any more food. So she gave him a bottle. He enjoyed it and drifted off to sleep.

Martha bought James Jr. a walker and began putting him in the little walker. As she did this, she noticed that his little legs were getting stronger. Her mother told her that she needed to be careful with little boys because they were very, very curious, and to make sure she put things out of reach of James because he would touch everything once he started walking. So, Martha listened initially but soon forgot about it.

James Jr. learned how to walk. "Oh my Lord," Martha said, "What am I going to do with you? Every time I look up, you're grabbing something off the table and you're messing with the outlets." She laughed at him. She would say, "I'm going to put him in the bassinet." Next thing you know, he was climbing up out of the bassinet. So, she put it up a little higher to prevent him from climbing out of it.

James had been laid off from work, so Martha found a job. She went back to the hospital to continue her work there as a registered nurse. When she came home, she would fix dinner for James. He had just been hired for a new factory job. It paid some pretty good money. He still would not pay any attention to Little James Jr. Little Karen monopolized her father's attention. On their birthdays, grandmothers would send money. Five dollars would be sent to little Karen, and Little James Jr. would receive a dollar. This bothered Martha because she wanted her children to be treated equally. "James Jr., don't worry; everything you are not receiving from people, God is going to make sure he provides it to you." Martha would tell him. Martha went on and spoke to James about it. He told her, "I can't give him money. Move on!" Martha was troubled by this.

Martha noticed that little James Jr. had something different about him. For example, one day, when Martha went to his bedroom to tuck him in, he hugged her and said, "Mommy, it'd be okay, it be okay, I love you." She cried, and she said, "I love you too, baby." When James Jr. went to sleep, every time he went to sleep, he'd laugh while he was sleeping. Then there was another time when he went to sleep; he said, "Mama, Mama, they're tickling my feet." Martha said, "James Jr., go to sleep." So, he just went to sleep. She knew that something was different, but she had no idea what was about to happen in this whole ordeal.

happened?" she said. They both thought she was overreacting. However, this caused her to watch James Jr. much more closely.

Another thing they noticed about him was that he was extremely clumsy. He was always falling and pulling on things. Additionally, every time James Jr. was on his way to sleep, something would happen which would cause him to pull the cover up over his head. So Martha asked him one day, what was wrong? James Jr. said, "When you leave out, they are running around my bed, and they tickle me." She said, "Who, baby?" "My friends, said James Jr." And Martha said, "What friends?" James Jr. said, "The ones that are in my dream. They are here in this room."

Martha looked at him but ignored him and laughed at him. She said, "Baby, that is just your imagination." He said, "No, Mommy, they are here. They are like light, and; they run around. They chased me in my dreams. We have a lot of fun." Martha said, "You are probably dreaming about your sister Karen." And he said, "No, Mommy, these are my angels." She stopped and looked at him? Martha did not say a thing. She

Chapter 3
Life Changing

James Jr. was a very, very curious young man. One day, when James Jr. was three years old, he reached into the fishbowl and pulled out the fish. No one ever knew what happened to the fish. They said James Junior ate the fish.

Another day, Karen, James Sr., and Martha were looking for him all over the house. They kept calling for James Jr., but he was nowhere to be found. Suddenly, as they were looking around, James Sr. went to the refrigerator to get something to drink. He opened the door, and there he was, little James, at the bottom of the refrigerator in the chocolate cake. Everyone started to laugh, and Martha was very disturbed because she thought he could have suffocated in the refrigerator. "You guys are here, laughing? Do you have any idea what could have hugged him and told him to go to sleep. So, off to sleep James Jr. went.

The next day his mother got up for work. As she was leaving home, she went to see little James Jr. off. She said, "Alright, I am getting ready to go to work. Daddy is already at work. We will see you guys later." And he said, "Okay, Mom. Love you." His mother replied, "I love you, too, baby." So, Martha went off to work. Little James went back to sleep. The babysitter came over to watch the kids. The babysitter would always be on the phone. Every time little James needed something, she would look at him and get it for him. She would also give him something to eat.

Little James would sit in the chair and eat his lunch, and then he would go and play. He loved playing outside.

One day, he was playing on his big wheel, and little Karen was playing on her bike. In a moment, the kids decided to trade. Karen gave him her bike, even though little James did not know how to ride it. Little James Jr. turned the bike over. He saw that the babysitter was looking, and she asked James to turn the bike back over. She looked at him and walked away. James Jr. turned it back over again, not listening to her. He started spinning the bike wheels harder and harder, and he stuck his finger in the bicycle spoke. James' finger was cut clean off. Little Karen was screaming and crying because little James' finger got severed. When he looked at his finger, he passed out. Quickly, the babysitter hung up the phone and called 911. Once James' mother arrived home, she ran across the street to see what was going on, but the ambulance had come by that time.

They were looking for the finger and could not find it, so they patched him up and put him in the ambulance. James looked up as the paramedic was standing over him. When he looked up, he passed out again. When little James finally woke up, he was in the hospital, and his mom was standing over him. It was the same hospital where she worked. His uncles and everyone were standing over him when he passed out again.

James had a life-changing moment while he was in

surgery. James Jr. was out for two and a half weeks. The doctors had no idea what had happened. Even though it was just his little finger, he had lost quite a bit of blood. He went into shock and was out for two and a half weeks.

While he was out the two and a half weeks, his mom sat in his room praying and reading the Bible to him. James Sr. was nowhere to be found. Martha was getting very troubled because her child needed blood. Everyone was trying to give him blood, but they were not the right match.

When James finally came, the one thing he found was that this child was his. All this time he thought that this child was not his, and then he had to give him blood.

Once James Jr. woke up, his mother and his father were there. They said, "We thought we were going to lose you. What happened?" And he told his mother, "Mommy, I was looking at you guys. Every time that you cried, He told me to tell you, it is going to be okay." Martha replied, "Who told you that James Jr.?" "Michael." And she said, "Michael, who?" "That is my angel, Mommy."

Startled, she looked at him with a stare. Then she said, "What else did he tell you?" "He showed me the world. We walked around, and we are the same age, walking around. He was talking with me, and we were having fun in the sandbox. Finally, he told me it was time for me to go. Then I laid down on the bed, and I woke up, and you guys were here."

When his father heard it, he looked at him but did not understand what was going on and why. He had so many questions going through his mind. He thought his son was suffering from brain damage. So Martha called her mother to find out what she thought was going on with him. Martha's mother told her that James Jr. was very, very special. He is more special than she knew. Martha's mother said, "Reading the Bible had nothing to do with you. It had everything to do with him."

James Jr. continued to grow. Finally, the time came when he and his sister started school. Their parents chose to put them in private school. Little James Jr. and Karen had no idea why they were going to that school. They wanted to go to the regular school with all the other kids, but James Sr. did not want them to. Little Karen wanted to go and play with everyone. Karen had a feisty little spirit, and every time she went somewhere, she wanted to fight. She wanted to fight the little kids in school, and she wanted to fight the teacher. She wanted to do some of everything.

When little James Jr. was in school, he would look down the hall to see who was coming. James Junior could feel when his father was in the school. His father would bring them lunch. He asked the teacher if he could go to the restroom, and she let him go. He saw his dad walking down the hallway, and he shouted, "Dad!" "What are you doing in this hallway?" his dad asked. James Jr. said, "I don't know. I just knew you were coming here." James Sr. had no idea little James Jr. was so gifted.

When James Sr. looked in little Karen's classroom, she was sitting in the corner with her hair all over the place. He found out that little Karen had an altercation with a teacher. So he took her into the restroom, tore her up, took her back to class, and made her apologize to the teacher in front of the class. He finished by telling her to sit down and not do anything else.

As time went on, Martha and James started having marital problems. Because they had no idea what was going on in their lives, they separated. James stayed in Indiana. Martha went back home to Illinois where she stayed with her sister. She soon found a place of her own and began working for Kohl's Department Store. Martha worked for Kohls for a very long-time selling shoes. In this season, while she was working, the children missed their father badly. Little James would ask her when they were going back home. Martha replied, "We're going home in time." Whenever Martha went to see her sister, Louise, her sister loved Little James Junior. She favored him so very much. Anything that little man wanted, she gave him. She knew little James loved to eat. So every time he was hungry, she told him that she was his second mom and whatever he wanted to eat, she gave it.

One day, his aunt's husband, Watty, asked James Jr., "You want to go fishing?" James Jr. said yes, and so he took him fishing. While he was out there on the boat with Uncle Watty, his uncle told him to stop standing up because he would fall in the water. As little James threw the fishing rod out into the water, he fell in the water with it. His uncle jumped in after him and pulled him out of the water. He said, "Son, I told you not to get in the water." Little James said, "But, I caught a fish." His uncle told him, "I know, but you should have left it for me." They went home with a few fish and he showed Aunt Louise that he caught a small fish. She cooked the fish for him, and he ate them. One day, Aunt Louise and Martha had an argument. They were distraught with each other. James Jr. cried, "I want to go home to my daddy." Martha just looked at him. Louise told Martha, "I think you should take them home." So, she got on the bus and took them back home.

There was something different that Martha had to see when she got home. When she arrived, she found out James had become saved. He had been going to church and when she got home, the house was spotless from room to room. This was unusual for James Sr. After that, every day, they went to church as a family. They went to Bible study, and they went to prayer meetings. In this church, there was a pastor whose name was Pastor Guidens. One day, he walked up to James Jr. when he was about nine years old. He asked him if he was the son of James Sr. James Jr. said' "Yes, sir, I am." The pastor said, "Let me ask you a question," James replied, "Yes sir." "When are you going to preach, preacher?" And little James looked at him and laughed. He answered, "What do you mean?" and went on his way.

As time went on, James was in school and things started to change in his life. His little sister never played with him. Karen was very feisty. Karen often got into fights with people. Little James could not understand why, and when she wanted to go outside, she would go and ask her mother. Martha would say no. She would then go ask her father. He would ask Karen what did her mom say? And Karen would say, "Mom said come and ask you." James Sr. said, "Are you guys done with your chores?" Karen said, "Yes, sir." So, he said that they could go outside. Little Karen would go back inside and tell Little James, "Dad said we can go outside." Little James said, "I thought mom said we couldn't?" There was this back and forth about whether they could go outside and play. Then they found out that little Karen was playing them against each other.

Soon James and his sister joined the choir. Their mother and father took over the junior choir because the other director was becoming feeble and older. When they took over the choir, they went and picked up all the little kids. The choir was huge. When little James began singing, he performed a solo. Everyone loved it. "He is going to be special," said the pastor.

One day after church service was over, Little James was on the way out the door when the pastor walked up to him and tapped him on the shoulder. James Jr. turned around and looked up to him and said, "Sir?" The Pastor asked, "When are you going to preach, preacher?" Little James just laughed and walked away.

James later went home and went to sleep. He had a dream. In his dream, someone told him, "It is time for you to be baptized so that you can come even closer." Little James told his father that he had to be baptized. His father asked him, "Why?" "Because the Lord told me it's time." The following Sunday the Pastor opened the doors of the church and started accepting people for baptism. James Jr. was afraid to go up front by himself. So, he laid down on the pew. His father came around and picked him up. Little James broke out in tears. The pastor said to the congregation, "You guys don't know. I just came back from the Holy Land, and the Lord told me this young man is going to speak to the nations." The Pastor started praising God. He said that is the reason why he kept walking up to him. The following Sunday James got baptized. The Pastor told him everything that was going to happen. When James went into the water, he noticed something different about himself. He could see and hear things that he had never heard before. His life was changing.

Chapter 4
Everything New

Now, as for James, there were all of these that were tapping in his life. He knew there was something different now. All of a sudden, he had this desire to read his Bible. He began reading, but he had no idea where to start. He had been attending Sunday school every Sunday. His mom taught Sunday school, and he was in the class. He asked so many questions every time there were Sunday school lessons. Even in Bible study, he had questions. When he was in Bible study class, he would ask questions that they could not answer. He knew that there was something different. He would ask the Deacons who were teaching, but no one could answer his questions about the scriptures as they were written. His father told him that he was in class to listen. Just hear what they had to say. James said, "I cannot understand why they will not answer my questions every time I ask." James Jr.'s dad told him just to listen and learn. James told him he would.

While James Jr. was in school, he always wanted to do good. He also wanted to play with his sister, but she had no desire to play with him. She used to call little James crazy because he would say, "You don't have to play with me. My friends will play with me." The whole time that James was in school Karen would always get into fights. She would run to her little brother James and ask for help. James would always help his big sister no matter what. However, Karen would leave him by himself and play with her friends. As James was growing up, he tried to make friends. However, his friends would bully him, mess with him, and not want to be his friend. Little James would just find something else to do like walk around outside. He would just watch people play.

When he went to high school for the first time, he liked a little girl. He really, really liked her. So, he started talking with her. He thought to himself, she has the same spirit that I do. Her name was Gina. He was very crazy about Gina, but suddenly Gina's mom got sick, and they moved away. Little James was very hurt because the only friend he had moved away.

As time passed, James moved up in school. Little James loved to run and Karen was very fast. So James Sr. put them in summer track and field. Though Little James was very short, he really desired to win. He announced that one day he was going to win. James continued to run. He joined the High School track team and won one race. One boy teased James and said that James won the race because he was not running.

James Jr. laughed at the boy and decided to ignore him. But then, he told his dad, James Sr., that he wanted to play football. His mother said, "No, you are not there to get hurt." James Sr. replied, "Let the boy play football. Let the boy play."

Little James was very short, like a bit of a runt. Most of the time, he just sat out there on the field. Everyone would get to play except for him. He would have on his little shoulder pads and shoes but would never get to go into the game. The Coach tried him out on the kickoff team. One day someone got hurt, so they put little James on the receiving team. He caught the ball effortlessly. They all looked at him as though he was a pro while he was running. James ran to the right; he ran to the left. He saw somebody was running after him and because he was so scared, he ran with all his might. James got a touchdown! His coach said to him, "Where did that speed come from? Come here, Lil' James!" Little James earned a spot on the kickoff team. James was placed in the backfield every time there was a kickoff in the middle of the field.

For some reason, even though he was short, he could catch the ball and run fast, but James wanted to be better. So, he asked his dad for help. His dad said, "What do you want me to do, little James?" James Jr. said, "Can you help me to get faster?" James Sr. said, "You sure this is what you want me to do, little James?" Little James replied, "Yes Sir." So, his dad took him to a park called Storyland Zoo that was full of hills. He said, "This is what I want you to do...run every one of these Hills." Lil James asked, "Do you want me to run up and down the Hills?" James Sr. said, "No, turn and run up the hills, and you when you get back down the hill, I want you to run back up the hill." Little James turned to his dad and said, "Dad, the hills are so steep. How am I going to make it to the top?" James Sr. said, "I want you to run with all your might to the top of these hills." Little James had determination. Because he was so close to the ground, every time he ran up the steep hills, it was like he was crawling up the hills. However, he was very determined to get up those hills. Little James put his mind to it and succeeded.

When it was time for the football game, he went to practice. His coach looked at him and said, "James Jr., run out there and keep running." He told the quarterback, Chris, to throw him the ball. Chris threw him the pass and little James caught it. The coach said, "Hmm." One day during the kickoff return, their star receiver pulled a hamstring at the end of the game." Coach called out to James Jr., but he was looking around. His teammates were saying to him, "Coach Badge is calling you." Little James heard them and replied, "Yes, sir." The Coach instructed him, "This is what I want you to do. I need you to run down the field in a straight line and turn around then reach out and catch the ball. I need you to run down the field, don't turn, don't look anywhere else, just turn around and catch the ball." Little James said, "Okay!" The coach gave him a count on three.

As there were 10 seconds left in the game, Chris went back to pass. James took off running. He was running at the same speed as the ball while Chris threw it downfield. James Jr. turned around and caught the ball in the end zone, and it was a touchdown. From that point forward, James's life changed. Suddenly, he went from the person who was no good to the star player on the team. And James was a star receiver. By the time he got to 10th and 11th grade, he was catching passes no matter where they threw the ball. There was a time when it was raining outside. James went back and they did a reverse and tossed him the ball. He cut down the field. The defense thought they were about to get him, and James ran for a touchdown.

Even though James Jr. was talented, one thing about him was that he was humble. He did not brag about who he was or how good he was. However, there was a little girl that James loved. Her name was Judy. He was crazy about Judy when they were in school, but Judy changed schools. While this really upset him, he remained in touch with her.

There was something different that was happening in James's life, and His mother noticed it. Every time he arrived at home before he did his homework, James would pray. Before he went to bed, he would pray. He would pray when he got up in the morning and when he was on the way to school, even while he was on the school bus. Karen would ask James Jr. was there something wrong with him because he would be sitting there talking to himself while on the school bus. James Jr. Would say, "Karen, I am not talking to myself. I am talking with someone." She never understood him. As time went on, Little James Jr. went about his way.

When he was playing football his senior year, his coach continued to tell James to stop jumping. One day James Jr. jumped up to catch a football at a game, a guy jumped down on him and James broke his kneecap.

Doctors told him that he would never walk if he got hit in his knee again. Little James Jr. was devastated. Some schools had been talking to him about playing college football. He felt like his life had ended.

The fortunate thing about James Jr. is that he was perfect in everything he did, even in his schoolwork. He almost got straight A's in high school. He had a grade point average of 3.67. Soon James Jr. graduated from high school and went to community college, and he then found work. The college was right next to Kroger's, where he worked as a bagger. While James was different, everything was about competition with him. He went to the same Junior College as Karen. James could not type like everyone else because his finger was cut off. However, he was given an electric typewriter to use, and he excelled.

James had become very close to his father in his teenage years and his father was extremely hard on him. He would tell him to stop playing around, to stop laughing, and to take life seriously. And while he would tell him things like life was not a game, James Jr.

understood his father. This made James strong. His father became his best friend.

One time, his father fell asleep while they were watching TV. James got up and said, "I am going to bed." Little James said good night. James Sr. went to sleep. Even though Little James had his own room upstairs, he decided to remain on the couch downstairs. He had a very uneasy feeling. His father made a noise after he went to sleep, and he could not figure out what was wrong with him. He kept hearing his mother Martha say, "James, turnover!" She turned on the light and looked at him. His eyes were opened while he was making this noise. She said to James, "James!" Instantly, Little James ran upstairs to see what was going on. He saw that his father was a shell. He was gone. Suddenly, he got on top of his father and started giving him CPR as he learned it in class. They called 911 and the police came and proceeded to administer CPR.

The paramedics arrived and took over the CPR. While the paramedics were administering CPR, Martha was running all over the house, saying, "What am I going to do? Where is he at? I am losing my best friend." The paramedics tried to do all they could. They put Little James out of the room. While he was walking, his uncle came to him. He said, "Son, I know this is hard for you. I am going to be here for you. But the paramedics want to know what you guys want to do." And James said, "What do you mean?" His uncle continued, "Your dad is just holding on with a little bit of life. They want to know if you want them to continue to resuscitate him." Little James Jr. said, "I don't know. Continue to try." They tried. However, their efforts were unsuccessful, so they stopped. James Jr. was heartbroken. A day or so had gone by when James went outside, stood on the porch, looked up at the sky, and said, "My dad is gone. The only thing I have is you now because I have no one else. Please don't leave me. please don't leave me."

The family buried their father. Martha had a hard time dealing with her husband's death. Karen was a daddy's girl, so she was having tremendous problems. As Karen became an adult, she had a boyfriend that helped ease every bit of pain she was experiencing about her father's passing. Everyone turned to James Jr. to be the man of the house. He had no idea what to do. The only thing he knew was that he would be going to work and school.

His mom and sister did not get along. One day, while listening to them, Lil James told his sister that he would help their mother to stop. So, he signed for Karen to go to school. As time went on, Little James would go to school, work, come back home, and go to church. At church, he asked, "Why do I not hate going to that church anymore? Because of the church, I changed." He told her, "I need more." And he said, "I need more. It is not enough for me." So, James started going to other churches to make it more.

Martha noticed something different about little James. She felt like he was pulling away from her. One day James went to sleep, and in his dreams, the Lord said to him that he wanted him to leave his house and go to a land he would show him. So James enlisted in the Army. His mom asked him, "Why are you leaving?"

He said, "Because the Lord told me that I must leave and go to a land where he will show me." With that, she said, "okay," and little James left.

Chapter 5
Beginning A Journey

Before little James decided to go to the Army, he began looking back over his life, remembering how he had been denied and how everyone did not accept him. He was looking over those things and could understand what God was doing in his life. James began to understand why he was being taken away from his family. He was concerned about his mother Martha since it had been just four years since his father passed away. James was very concerned because he had never been away from home before. During that time, he was with his friends, but he never had a chance to mourn. He had been consumed with being there for his mother and sister to make decisions. He was only 19 years old.

He had no idea what to do or what to say. He did not know what was right or what was wrong. He would just try to make the best decisions he knew how to make. It was during this time that he went on into the military. Little James was stationed in Fort Knox, Kentucky. He was in the resting area just before they came and to get him for basic training. As he was sitting there, he saw four of the drill sergeants come in yelling and screaming. They were trying to get them up early to ready the recruits for what was to come. Lil James got afraid.

After dinner, James called home. The sergeants had taken away everyone's phones so they could not talk to anyone. He made a collect call home to his mom and told her, "Mom, I want to come back home." She said, "No! The Lord told you to go there and you must stay there. I'm proud of you. You're going to make it! This will change your life forever. You're not little James anymore. Your father has passed. You are not James Jr. You are James now. I'm proud of you. I want you to make me proud of you. I want you to go in here and do everything God is telling you to do."

James went back to the barracks where he was staying. The day arrived when they came to get him and all the other recruits that were there. They called them soldiers. As they got them all up out of bed, they told them to get on the truck. They had gotten them uniforms and everything. When they got on the truck, they went to the other side of the base. During that day it was raining, and suddenly, it happened. They were on the truck when they moved back to the quilt on the truck. The sergeants yelled for everyone to get off the truck. All the recruits were trying to hurry off the truck grabbing their bags and stuff. The sergeants wanted everyone to stand on the line, but no one knew where the line was because it was pouring down rain. "You have 10 seconds to get up the steps," they were told. "Ready, go!" So everyone started running up the steps. All of a sudden the sergeant said, "10,7,5,1, get down get, down get, down get, to the ground! Push the ground! Push the ground! Do push-ups!" Every time that they missed, they had to go back out there.

James was getting frustrated because he did not understand. They told James to put his rucksack on his back. The drill sergeant would sit on his back as he started to do push-ups. James was trying to do push-ups, but he couldn't because a man was sitting on his back. As James continued, the sergeant told everybody to toe the line. This time the sergeant gave them 25 seconds to get up the steps. Mind you, they had to be on the third floor. Suddenly, they began counting again. "25, 15, 10…" Everyone was running up the steps. James was so excited because he made it up to the steps and the barracks quickly. They all worked as a team with no one left behind. Finally, the sergeant yelled, "Get outside, get outside!" This frustrated James because everyone was outside in the pouring rain doing push-ups.

James was regretting that day and the decision that he had made. All of a sudden, the sergeant said, I will give you 30 seconds to get upstairs! Because everyone thought that 30 seconds was a long time, they all looked at each other and started pulling each other along. They said you know that they are not going to give us 30 seconds. So, when they started counting, everyone was rushing up the steps. This time, they all made it. They told them to tow that line.

When they were in basic training, the first weeks were the roughest times James had ever gone through. He learned, even though he was in good shape, he had never run four and five miles before. James had never climbed a mountain before, jumped from a plane, or propelled out of a helicopter before. He was also learning to shoot take care of his rifle. Each time he was done shooting, he had to clean it. Even though James was a perfectionist, he had to learn new things in a greater depth than he had ever known.

James missed home so badly, and he was always wondering how his mom was doing. So, he started writing his mom letters. He even wrote his mom five letters in one week. James kept wondering why she never wrote him back. Finally, three weeks later James received one letter. He wondered why the dates were so far off. Then his answer came. The sergeants told James that no one got letters for the first two weeks of training. They wanted the recruits to remain at a certain emotional level.

As James continued to train, he reached a point

where he had to go to the gas chamber and then complete all the physical training tests. James did exceptionally well on his physical training test and was ultimately awarded a patch. In addition, because he performed very well shooting his weapon, he received all the badges.

As James maintained, he called his mom in the sixth week and told her he was soon to graduate. He informed her of his graduation day and James' family attended his graduation. At the graduation, James looked at his sister and noticed that she was a little big. So he asked her, "What is wrong with you, Karen? You look a little big?" She said, "I'm pregnant." Not knowing what else to say, James looked at her and said, "Wow." Afterward, they all went to dinner.

Once graduation had ended, and James had spent time with family, he went to his Advanced Individual Training. He actually enjoyed that training. He had never experienced any training like that before. It was so much fun to him that the only thing he knew was how to have fun. He was training to learn his job, but he had fun doing it. The only thing James thought about was, "Wow, this was a great relief," he would say to himself. He said, "Man, this is only for four weeks." He was wondering what he should do next after the training. James was given the option to go home for a vacation or go straight to his permanent party.

James decided that he was going to go home to spend time with his mom and sister. Upon arrival, he went over to his sister's house to see what she was doing. James enjoyed spending time with Karen. Then he went to spend time with his mom. Martha showed James all over the city. She was excited to tell everyone that her son was in the military and was a serviceman of the United States Army. His mom said to him, "James, I'm so proud of you I don't know what to do."

Once his time visiting with his family was done, James returned to his permanent party. He had no idea what was about to happen to him. His life had changed. James' mom told him not to forget to look for a church home. He replied, "I plan to, Mom." So, as promised, James started looking for a church home. He went down to the chapel, but he said, "No, that's not enough. This is too quiet." So James asked around and went to another church. This time, it was a Baptist Church. This church still was not enough for him. Then he found a friend one night that he thought would be taking him out. Instead, the friend invited James to the Friday night service. As he was sitting there, he was very curious about what kind of church it was. It was a non-denominational church, which he had never been to before. His friend told him it was a Holiness Church. When he went to church, he was used to devotion and other things like that. At this church, they had praise and worship, and suddenly they began worshipping God. James was all into it, and he wanted more.

So, when bible study and prayer meetings were there, he was there. When there was a church service, he was there. Sunday school? He was there because, during this time, James started getting more excited about this church. When it was time for prayer, the pastor asked did anyone need prayer? Since James wanted more from God, he was always up there for prayer. He said, "Whatever I can get from Him, I want it. I don't care what it is. I just want more from Him because I love Him." That is all James kept saying. The thing about it, no one had accepted James. His friend that brought him was 6'7, 236 lb. He was tall and light-skinned. It seemed like the whole church liked him more. Every time he went up for prayer, they had a Word for him, all the time. James would just sit there, watch, and say, "Lord, you don't have anything for me?" That is all he kept saying. He said, "Lord, you don't have anything for me." He kept wanting and wanting, "Lord, just speak to me." However, he did not get anything.

James continued to come to the church, and then one day, something happened. They had said they were going to have an all-night prayer meeting. James said, "I am going because I want something from God. I am going to pray; I am going to keep praying until my change comes. I know God is going to tell me something." So he spoke this thing, and he said, "Imma keep praying until God hears me!" James had no idea what was about to happen in his life due to the words he spoke.

During this time, his military base had gone on alert and expected to go to Desert Storm. James was so afraid; there was so much uncertainty. He said to himself, "Man, am I about to die." He asked, "Lord did you bring me all the way over here, and I'm going to war?" While he was sitting there praying, everyone else had their own partners. He stooped down on a chair, and it was just him and God. And he started to pray. During that time, James really knew how to pray. He had learned from listening to his father and listened to what his pastor said. The Lord had given him words to pray. When he started to pray, he suddenly shut his eyes and heard something like a metallic click. As his eyes were shut in the dark, it seemed like a white quilt covered him, and it became light. From the top of his head to the soles of his feet were covered with light. This experience stretched him out on the floor as though he was on the cross.

He spoke with many tongues. Suddenly, he was out of his body, and he could see himself. He saw the pastor come over and put her hand on his stomach. Things happened, and it was finished. The pastor told him that he was not going over to the war, for this war. "You are not going over there to fight." "You're going over to see Him and to learn about Him. Your life will never be the same." That was the first word that the pastor had ever given to him. James did not understand at that moment what had happened to him. He had an out-of-body experience looking at himself while speaking in tongues. He didn't tell anybody when it happened because he did not know what to say.

James was going to Saudi Arabia. He said goodbye to his mom and everyone who came over to see him off. He was so afraid. Once again, he had no idea what was about to occur. When he got to Saudi Arabia, he commented that it was hotter than he had ever seen it before. It was 136 degrees outside and in the shade, it was 126 degrees. He asserted how it was so hot that sweat was running off his forehead. Sweat was coming from everywhere, even in the shade. So, James said, "I have got to get some water." They told him that everyone had to have one box of water. There were six waters in each box. They instructed them that they needed to drink six waters per day. Mind you, these containers held two liters of water each. James wanted to keep his water cold, so he decided to dig a hole and put the water down in the hole and cover it. Everyone was looking at him, wondering why was he doing that? "This will keep the water cool," he said. He did not like drinking hot water. The water was cooler, so everyone else started doing the same thing.

They finally reached a place where they could stay with air conditioning in each of the rooms. James looked and saw that the war in Iraq had already begun when they were attacking Kuwait. James was so afraid because he thought this was what would happen to them. He went into the room and asked, "You guys want to have a prayer meeting or read the Bible?" They ignored him. So, he went on and committed that he would pray by himself. James went into his room and turned down his air and began to read. James' mom had told him that whenever he was afraid to open the Bible to Psalms 91. So, he started to read that. James laid down and prayed. As he drifted off into sleep, he kept hearing something in his room. He looked but did not see anything. So, he turned back over, and as soon as he turned over, he heard something like a lion roaring. He heard the lion call him by name. "James! James! Be not afraid. I have chosen thee." James tried to turn over, but he could not move. The only thing that he could do was cry. The voice said, "James, James, be not afraid. I am Jesus." The only thing James knew how to do in that moment was cry. He told him that his cry was heard. "I see your desire and the love that you have for me. And you will speak to many nations. All that have rejected you have rejected me. I will see you again. My servants will hear again. They will walk again. All that you believe it shall be." Finally, He said, "Just believe."

During this time that he was speaking to James, he put him under a waterfall. Water was flowing all over him. And on the bottom of his feet, he was walking through the Bible and the pages of the Bible were turning. It was filling him as he spoke. He continued to listen to God. His presence was so strong, James could not stop crying and listening. He said to the Lord,

"Lord, I love you with everything in me. And I will go wherever you want me to go. I will say whatever you want me to say. I will die if it be your will." Jesus said, "I know. Since you were born, you were given the gift of love. It comes with a great deal of responsibility. And no one will accept you. Because what I have given you is unconditional, I need for you to give this to the world." James said to him, "I will. I will." And He said, "My son, every tear you have cried, I have it. Always remember this, even though man has rejected you, you are already accepted in heaven, and you will speak to many nations. You will speak to many kings. You will restore heavenly places to people who have no hope." James said, "I want to make sure that I stay humble before you." And He said to him, "I know you will. The love that has been placed on the inside of you has increased so much." And He said, "I must go. I will come again when the time comes." And James said, "Wait!" And He disappeared.

James immediately turned over and was looking for Jesus but could not find him. He looked all down the hallway and outside. His friends kept asking him,

"What's wrong? What's wrong? What happened?" He said, "I can't explain it." One of them said, "Tell me, man, what happened?" James said, "The Lord appeared to me!" He said, "What! Man, I thought you were going to say something." He did not believe him. James went on to sleep and he got up the next day. There was a guy that would always pick at his ears. While he was getting ready to hit James on the ear, James could see behind him. When he stepped into the shadow, he stepped back, and he changed his mind.

Chapter 6
Coming Into Understanding

James sees all these things that were happening to him. He understood and found out that he was rejected by man most of the time in his life. James could relate to the things that were happening to him because people rejected Jesus also. James loved the Lord Jesus so much that the Lord answered him because of his love. James was always listening to hear from the Lord. When he said, "Lord, I will do the work; whatever you want me to do, I will go wherever you want me to go; say whatever you want me to say." James meant everything in his heart because he loved the Lord. He loved the Lord with everything in him.

James began to listen to worship and praise songs all the time. He was lying on his bed, and there were other people in the room. James was sitting there with his eyes shut while everyone else was taking a nap. As

James was lying there, he began to worship and praise God; he had an out-of-body experience that pulled him out of his bed.

He went through the ceiling past the top of the earth past the stars. The Lord pulled him out there where everything was void. He showed him how it was at the beginning of time. As James came back down, he opened his eyes suddenly, and he was breathing hard and was looking around. The guy that was over across the room was still listening to music on his headphones. James was looking around as if something was wrong with him. James got up, went to lunch, and as he was walking around, he noticed something. He could see and hear differently. He heard things he never heard before. Now James was able to overhear what was in the people's hearts.

Later that day, after dinner, James decided to resume working. That's when he noticed someone having Bible study. James sat and listened to him. One of the teachers said, "Hey, would you like to say something?" James got up and spoke. When he spoke, everyone turned around. The Believers could not believe James was speaking. All of James' friends often wondered why James was so quiet. James rarely said anything. However, this time, the focus was on James. What happened? James' best friend looked at him. And tears started rolling down his eyes. And he looked at James, and later he said, you are God's anointed. And James looked at him and didn't say anything. He said there was a glow behind you. There was a gold glow. Everyone could see it, which is why we were looking at you the way we were looking at you. And it got brighter. The Lord is with you. And James didn't say anything; he continued to do what he was doing and stayed humble before the Lord. People were trying to understand how he learned the Word the way that he did. He was so fluent, and there was so much power and understanding. And then people were confused. Then he even went to church services that they had at the chapel. The pastor, the clergyman that was there, looked over at him. He didn't know him at all. He asked him if he would like to speak? James was astonished because he had no desire to speak. He was just there listening. And he got up and spoke to each one of them there.

As James spoke, he noticed one guy sitting there that would not look up. So James asked him what was troubling his heart? And the guy said, "I can't look at you because it's as if you're looking right at me, and I can't lie." And James, astonished, looked at him and said, "You don't have to be ashamed of anything. The Lord forgives you of all your sins." And so, when James went back to his room, he prayed. He asked God for greater understanding because he didn't want to get beside himself. He always told the Lord that he wanted to stay humble before him. So, as James was praying, he drifted off into a dream. As he drifted off in his dream, he was there on the beach with his friends. In James's dream, he was a kid. His friends were on the beach with him and walked away from saying they wanted to go inside. But James wanted to stay on the beach to watch the water hit the shore.

Suddenly, a man walked up to him and asked him, "Will you walk with me?" And James says, "Sure, I don't have anything else to do. And the men asked, why are you so discouraged? And James said no one understands me." And the man that was walking with him said, "no one understands me either, and they said, I know how you feel." James stumbled. And the man grabbed James' hand so that he would not fall. James thanked him. During this time in James' dream, he never looked up at the man. And suddenly, they started walking up the hill. While walking, James began to stumble more because the sandy Hill had become rock. As they were walking, James almost fell again. Suddenly, the man picked James up and carried him. As he continued to walk up this hill, the hill got steeper and steeper. Suddenly the man took one big step. James never looked up at him because he was too busy looking down to see what was under him.

When the man took the step, he stepped over a mountain and then stepped over another Mountain. During this time, he was talking to James. He was telling him all about the world. And many places that he would see and many people that he would speak to and many things he would have to do. And He said to him, many people have rejected me so they will reject

James responded, "Please come back, don't leave me!" The man said, "I will always be with you," and James cried, "Please, come back!" And he said, "Always be with you." Once again, He said, "I will always be with you, and he disappeared out of sight." And James said lastly, "Forgive me for not knowing who you were."

When James got up, he was in tears, and things had changed. Throughout this time of the war, James was ministering to people. Not only was he ministering to people, but people were getting saved and filled with the Holy Ghost. James and his friends continue to minister. Through that time, when the war started, James was afraid but not afraid. He had a moment of peace. And when he went to sleep, he feared nothing. Though a lot of chaos was going on during that time, every time James spoke to someone, their life was free. Even his friend that brought him to the church for the first time, recognized that God had touched his life. So, they went, and many people were saved.

When the war was over, it was time to go back home. While they were traveling, things were you. And then, suddenly, James was on the other side of the hill, and they were walking down the hill. James noticed the sand, and he said the sand is so peaceful, it's as if no one is there. And the man said to him, "What do you mean?" James said it's as though no one had been on the beach at all. He said, "It's because the water has washed the feet of people away." So he continued to walk with Him, and then He put them down. And they began walking and kept walking on the beach. Then, all of a sudden, James heard his friends call, but he ignored them. And the man said to James, "I must go," and James said, "Where are you going?" the man said, "I must go and see my father." James said, "Oh, I understand." The man said, "Don't worry, I will always be with you." And James said, "Huh? What do you mean, you'll always be with me?" Then he heard his friends call him again. This time James turned his head to look at his friends for a second. When James looked back, and the man let go of his hands. He looked up because he was looking around for him, and when he looked up, he saw Him as He was ascending to Heaven. James pleaded, "Please don't leave me!" He said, "I will always be with you."

happening even while James was on the plane. As they flew over the United States for the first time, James had a very sick feeling in the pit of his stomach, like he was going into a land of sickness. He did not like what he felt, so James ignored the feeling and came down. Once James was home, he went back to the same church as before. However, he sensed that he didn't need that church anymore, so he started looking for a different Church. James realized the church where he had gone before was not enough for him.

James and his friend searched to find a different Church, an Apostolic Church. This time James and his friends started looking and listening to the ways of the apostolic, walking the apostolic way. James already knew, as well as everyone who came across his path knew this about him. However, James remained humble. There were a lot of people arguing over the Bible in church. There was one young lady over there who kept getting upset in such a way that she ended up getting sick because James told her to stop arguing over the Bible. He also said that she would suffer the same fate as the young lady that she was arguing with. The young lady was so upset because she had a bad temper. She wanted to be right because she felt denied. James said to her, "You're not denied. Heaven accepts you so don't fret." She didn't listen to him. Suddenly, she broke out with sores from the top of her head to the bottom of her feet. The sickness was so bad they had to send her to Germany. She could not go back to the United States. At that time, her husband told James what happened. James spoke with her over the phone. And he asked her, "What have you learned?" Then he asked of her, "Please forgive me. Your sins are forgiven, and you are restored." Three days later, the doctors were stanched because they were trying to figure out what was happening and from where the sores had come. Suddenly, the sores were gone entirely. Even where they had pulled up the skin, it was as if there was nothing there. So, a couple of days later, they continued to do tests. And finding nothing, they sent her home. The lady was so excited because she saw the change that was about to happen in her life.

Chapter 7
Walking In The Work

As time went on, James started getting used to being back in the United States of America. He enjoyed being with his friends who were saved and had a converted life. James taught them the things they needed to know. He taught them the things that he had learned when he was over in the desert. James started to have many different experiences. One day, James went to see his mother because it had been a very long time since he had seen her. When he walked in, she looked at him with surprise and said, "James, it's as though I don't know you. When I look at you, I can tell that you have changed." James did not say anything. He just stared at his mother, Martha. Finally, James said, "Mom, I missed you." Martha replied, "I thought I was going to have to send the National Guard out to find you, even though you're in the army." They both laughed. He told his mother, "While I was over there, we were not allowed to call home."

The next day, the city had a parade and a banquet for James. As James was walking downtown with his mom, James saw a blind man sitting on the side of the road. The man was asking for food. Martha said, James, "leave the man alone." And James said, "No." He sent his mom into the store as they would be stopping by Subway to get something to eat. As James walked up to the man, he asked him, "What can I do for you?" The blind man told him, "I just want something to eat." and James said, "For me to get you something to eat, I need you to do something for me." The blind man responded, "What is this about?" James said, "I know that you can't see, but I need you to do something for me to go get something for you to eat, something greater." So, the man told James that he would do it. James said, "I'm going right into the store and I'm going to get you something to eat, but I want you to keep your eyes shut." As James went into Subway and purchased a meal for the homeless man, he brought it back out to him. James said, "I need for you to keep your eyes shut. I'm going to put this right in your lap."

The man asked him, "When shall I open my eyes?" James said, "When it's time." As James looked at him, he said, "Lord bless him, and keep him, and restore him as a man." Then, James walked away from him while the man was still sitting there with food in his lap.

As James walked away and got to the end of the corner, the man opened his eyes. The moment he opened his eyes, everyone turned around because they heard him screaming. "I can see, I can see, I can see Hallelujah!" The man dropped his food on the ground because he was so excited that he could see for the first time in his life. Then, the man roused, saying, "It was a man, there was a man. I can see!" And people were just looking at him. James turned around to look and continued to walk with his mom. As they walked on, his mother looked at him and said, "I noticed something about you. Your spirit is so humble." Her soul felt astonished for the first time in her life about her son. She didn't even know what to say except, "I'm filled with joy!" James responded, "Oh, Mom, can I ask you a question?" And she said, "Yes, James." He asked, "Why didn't you tell me?" Martha asked, "Why didn't I tell you what?" "That I was chosen," said James, and Martha said, "Baby, I knew that you were chosen when you were on the inside of me. You would never ever be still unless I read the word to you." Martha asked James, "What are your plans?" And James said, "To do God's will. That's the only thing that I desire." So, Martha remained quiet. They did not speak a word for a while.

A little while later, James went back to his base. As he spoke to many of the people there, many of them desired to have Bible study with him. But during that time, it was almost time for him to deploy. He made many friends, those who were saved, renewed, and people who had been healed. The way that James did things was in secret. No one knew what was going on with these miracles. James was happy. One of the subjects James was teaching on was restoration. He also taught about how your past can affect your present future. He told his story of how everyone turned away from him, and no one accepted him. He spoke of how he was either too short or too small. He wasn't like everyone else. James told everyone when you see that things are happening in your life, even though men reject you, God'll always accept you. And that's the greatest acceptance there is. He continued to tell them that the world has a love that is conditional. And what you do for them, you cannot get back from them. If you don't do anything for them, you won't get anything from them. So, it's a love that's always conditional. God loves regardless. Because He is love - the Greatest Love of All. So as James continued to speak, many were broken on the inside.

James had one thing he yearned for; he had God's love, but he wanted a mate. But as hard as he tried to find someone, he couldn't find the person designed for him. Every time he was with someone, they would do something. He already knew it was going to happen. He remembered when he was dating one young lady, she asked to use his car. And James, with his giving heart, went ahead and allowed her to use the car. But she had a motive. She took James' car and went out with another man. When she called, James was sitting at home. He knew what she was going to do. And when James told her about it, she got upset because she thought that James had someone following her. But he didn't. She had no idea with whom she was speaking.

As time went on, James decided to continue to do God's will with it in his heart that God would send him that special person when the time came. He said, "Lord, I want them to understand me as I understand you."

So as James going on, the only thing he did was serve God, speak to people, restore people. People were getting saved and filled with the Holy Ghost. And there were many followers. Who was really wondering about this church? God told him the church is on the inside of you. It's on the inside of you. So this that I give you, I want you to go out, and I want you to give it to someone else. Help someone else's life to be restored. James's life was always busy because people called all the time during the day. James was growing tired. He could not get any rest. So one day, James decided that he was going to turn his phone off at night. He went to sleep. When turning his phone on the following day, he noticed that his voice mail was so full. People were calling as soon as he woke up. They couldn't understand why they couldn't reach him. The voicemail was full. James said, I just needed some rest. They laughed at him, saying, "Please forgive us. We talk so much; you have spoiled us. And then you turned your phone off, so we couldn't talk to you." James laughed.

James' life was such a beauty to the world. James once said, "I wish the world could see the love of God the way that I see it. I wish that everyone could see love the way they do during Christmas time. When they have the love of giving, and everyone is celebrating Christ. I wish that we could do this every day." When James celebrated Christmas, he really, really celebrated Christmas. He told everyone that he enjoyed Christmas more than his birthday. And they asked him why. James would tell them, "It's my Savior's birthday - my Savior that chose me to touch and bring his people home."

Chapter 8
Following the Vision of Jesus Christ

Now that James sees what's going on, he understands the reasons why Jesus chose him to do his work and his will. James set out to follow the vision that Jesus had given him. James understood that he was rejected and pushed to the side even as a child. As James grew up, things were happening to him. Everyone James talked to what not accept him. He could not understand while he was growing up why these things were occurring. However, the one thing James could see was that in his childhood, if these things had not have happened to him, he would not be able to have had a testimony to give to the people that could restore them. James could quickly identify with those who were broken. James would see people in ministry that would be going the wrong way. They would break out and go into ministry with brokenness. They would transfer that spirit into the next person that was already broken. So James set out to speak to the leaders, talk to them, and let them know that Jesus loves you first. James said, "No matter what it takes, I'm going to touch God's people and bring them back to Him because I gave Him my word." Even then, James was not accepted, but it didn't bother him because he loved Jesus so much that nothing could move him.

No matter what obstacle came his way, he kept pressing forward. When James spoke the Word to people, it didn't matter who they were, they would be restored. James would encounter many ministries that were big but battered in Christ. James would get phone calls from other churches to come and speak with the people to help them to restore the people. James would tell the people, from the Leaders, Bishop, the Apostles, the Prophet, to the Pastor, that first, we have to restore the Head. If you can't restore the Head, the whole body will die. When they had their leadership meetings, he would teach them to talk and pray together. James would give them one scripture that went with restoration, 2 Chronicles 7:14, "If my people who are called by My name would humble themselves and pray, seek My face, turn from their wicked ways, and then I will hear from Heaven. I will forgive their sins and heal their lands…"

First, we must repent and humble ourselves before the presence of God. James said that most people just come to God with a "just asking for something" attitude. They don't know how to surrender. That person ends up going back into the same thing that they just got rid of. It's like when you give your life to Christ for the first time; you're surrendering everything that has occurred in your life. You're laying it at the cross. James said to them, "Jesus died on the cross that we might be free. He died on the cross, that we may be able to come to Him." James was so passionate about it, that every time he spoke, he drew people to him.

When James came into different ministries, the people would draw close to him and would turn away from their pastors. They would turn away from their bishops. They would turn away from their Apostles. The men and women of God would get upset with James, saying," You're taking away my people." James responded by saying, "These people don't belong to any of us. They belong to God. I'm not taking anything from you. The only thing I'm doing is providing what God has given for me, to give to them." "Please, understand that I came in here to do my Father's will, and you invited me to do it. The people are thirsty for water. They are hungry for food. They're burning for God's will. They need the love of Christ in their lives because they have been battered, bruised, and rejected." As James spoke to the clergy, he told them that he understood them because they have been rejected just like he was rejected. "That's the reason why he called me to tell you to come to this place, to help you to restore His people," James told them not to give up, because he loved them, and he was going to stay right there with them, regardless of the circumstances. He also told them that the Bible says to be in the world, not of the world. As men and women of God, they needed to separate themselves from the world because they were trying to blend in with the world. He reminded them that this is the trick of the enemy. He said, "The enemy is tricking us, causing us to sabotage souls because we're blending in with the world. We wonder why we can't keep them? We're not living the authenticity of what God has said. We come up with excuses, but the Bible says that we are without excuse. We keep saying that we all fall short of the glory of God, but we keep using excuses. The Bible says that we are without excuse. We are not willing to repent and admit that we have done wrong and are lost. The only thing we have to do is come back to the remembrance of our beginning. Once we get to our beginning, we become new again. Pouring out all of the old things, and all things become new."

As they heard James speaking, they became excited. They repented themselves. They heard him. One of the things he said in the beginning, was," He who has an ear, let him hear what the Spirit of the Lord is saying to the church...your soul, so the change can come. Be set free from the bondage and the trickery that the world has given you. Jesus love you." James told them that whatever he had to do to help them to get to the finish line, he was going to do it. He did not care how much time it took to accomplish the goal. He was dedicated to helping them complete it. James wanted it done. James kept saying to the Lord that he needed so much help. There are so many people in the world that are battered. There are so many people that are bruised and put down. They're rejected and crying out. The Lord then spoke to James and said," Go and find me the biggest building." He said, "I will show you." He said, "Put your hands on it. Lay your hands on this building, and I will give this building to you."

James searched for many years, trying to find the right building. Then, one day, he drove up to that building. He laid his hands on that building as he had been instructed. God told him that He was going to give that building to him. James was waiting on God to give him that building while he continued to work on restoring souls. With the passion and the love he had in his heart, he wanted everyone to feel the love of Christ as he felt it. He would tell everyone his testimony about when he first met Him. He said, "I wish you could see as I see." One bishop asked James, "How do you see?" James answered and said, "Honestly, I can't see as everyone anymore." He said, "I even tried glasses, and I still can't see as everyone else sees." "I don't understand what you mean," said the bishop. James said when he saw the Lord, he changed his eyesight. "I don't see the flesh; I see the heart. I'm on a mission until death to gather God's people. Not only in the United States, but through the whole world. I must show everyone that God is Love. He is Love, and He has not forgotten us."

So many people try to love in so many ways. If they would first learn to love Christ, even the divorce rates would be lower. There would not be as much violence in the world if we would first learn the love of Christ. James said that his heart hurts every night when he prays and thinks of how many people are lost. His heart hurts when he sees people on the side of the road hungry and thirsty. They need food. They are homeless and hopeless. He said his heart aches when he walks through the store, feeling the people, and the only thing they need is love. His heart hurts from the deception presented by the church, where the people don't even want to attend anymore because of how the church has treated them. James told them that when they come to church, not to look at the person. Instead, listen to the Word that God is saying.

Chapter 9
Understanding The Vision

As James started to look back over his life, the why and the how and the where. Every other thing had been filled in. He understood why the Lord chose him to do this work. So, James wrote the vision down and made it plain that everyone he spoke to could understand. They wouldn't be confused about or ask questions about it. The only thing they would need to do when it came to their life is to decide what they were going to do once they find out that their past has affected their present. If they didn't do anything about it, it would impact their future. James spoke like this, "In my findings of Jesus Christ, I always asked the question of, why? Why did He choose me?" I know that in my life, I have been rejected by many, but I was accepted by Him, and He is the greatest Love of ALL."

We are all born into this world with innocence as a

baby. If we could just illustrate and not forget that innocence and humbleness as a child, the reembrace would make us a greater person. As we grow up and become adults, we start thinking independently and feel we can do whatever we want. Because God gave us a choice in the Garden of Eden, we had a choice to do His will. When it comes to love, it is unconditional if you get it from Jesus Christ. Love requires quite a bit of sacrifice. When it comes to love, people will come to you with all types of love. They will tell you if you love me, then I'll do this for you. But, when it comes to Jesus when you love Him, He will love you unconditionally.

You won't need to do anything but just love. He said, "If you love me, you will keep My Commandments." God loved us so much that He gave His only Begotten Son. So, when you think about how much He loves us, what man would lay down his life for a friend? The more that you put into God, the more you get out of Him. Some people only put a little into Him, and they only get a little out of Him because they have "time." They only have time for what they want.

When it comes to the love of God, what I have found was that He is the greatest love of all. Because He loved me so much, He gave me so many things, and I would rather have Spiritual things than natural things any day of my life.

When it comes to my life, me and my house, we serve the Lord in love. We give to people in love. No matter what it is, we give in love. I know there were times when I was persecuted because I love so much, and I love so deeply. I know that love is so deep that you cannot understand how far it can go. Think about how an eagle can fly to the highest height of the sky and get to the edge of the earth. He's able to see out into space. I think about how there is thin air up there.

When one considers the sea and how deep it is...there is also thin air down there. Love is the same thing. Love is thin air. There are only a few that want the love of God. To love Him comes at a price. There are things that one has to give up. Loving God is hard when one mixes personal desires with the pursuit of loving God. I've learned that through God's love, all things are possible. If you believe the love of Christ inside of you, nothing is impossible. You can reach the highest heights in life. Through His love and believing by faith, all things are possible. No matter what it is, it doesn't matter if someone is disabled. It doesn't matter if someone is sick. It doesn't matter what their situation says. All things are possible through Christ. Because of His love, He died on the cross for us.

Even while He was dying on the cross, there was still healing going on. We should think of how much someone could love us, to be healing still while dying on a rugged cross. Never forget what He has done for us and what we should be doing every day of our lives.

We should rededicate our lives and think back to when we were children when we didn't know evil. We would just play in the sandbox playing with our friends. For example, if a child pushed us, we would not be friends for a moment, but we would forgive and come back to play again.

We should continue to love and forgive. If we look in our past at all of the heartbreaks and disappointments with all of the things that have stopped life, we can start to blame. This is where bitterness sets in, and it becomes a roadblock. As you grow, that pain grows like a weed on the inside of you. You become more and more bitter. Then when you really try to love, it's hard because you lose the savor of the love Christ birthed in you when you were born. Once you find out that the thing deep on the inside of you is saying, "I'm trying to get there. I'm trying to love." You just have to surrender.

It's written that "If My people who are called by my name would humble themselves and pray, seek My face, and turn from their wicked ways," God said, "then I will hear from heaven, I will forgive their sins, and heal their lands." God wants us to humble ourselves as little children because we are His children. When we humble ourselves as little children, we can hear from Him. We can obey Him because we love Him. I remember when I was growing up, and I used to get in trouble with my mom and dad. I remember that even though I might have gotten in trouble, I knew that my mom and dad loved me. Because they loved me so much, it pushes me even today to give out the love that I had.

When Christ came to me and gave me the gift of love, that is the only thing that is on the inside of me. Through life and death, what I want to give is love. I'm not holding any bitterness on the inside because no matter what someone does to me, and no matter what someone says to me to hurt me, I still love them. When people hurt me, the only thing I say is, Lord, forgive them, for they know not what they do. What they don't understand is that when they persecute me, the only thing I give them back is LOVE. Amen.

Chapter 10
26th Year

Now James was in the 26th year of his life. He is out of the military, moving on, and adapting to civilian life. So it was pretty different for James as he moved on, you know. In contrast to life in the military structure, just being a civilian required a considerable adjustment to things around him. James had moved and wasn't in the same city as he was before. He started a Bible study, and he would talk to people about Jesus Christ to encourage them to convert and give their life to Jesus. He drew small crowds, and as the crowd got bigger, he assigned someone to that group, and he moved on.

James never wanted to draw attention to himself, and it was never his intention at all to ever, ever say that it's about him. There was a pastor that heard him speak. He asked him, "Brother James, how would you like to come over to my church and speak?" And James said, "Sure." However, James, at that time, did not know what was about to occur. So, James went over, and he spoke at the church and then.

As he spoke that night, the pastor asked him if he would come back the next night and for two additional nights. James told him that he didn't mind at all. He said, "It's not about me. It's about the blessings of the Lord Jesus Christ." So as he spoke the second night, there was another pastor that was there. He spoke to James, saying, "Brother James, what we need for you to do is when you get down here, we wanted to know if you would like to come over to our church and speak?" And James went on over and spoke at the other church. However, when he spoke at this church, they had him speak for seven days.

Now the one thing about James they could not understand is that he did not eat very much. And when he was preparing to minister, he would not eat at all because he would be fasting and praying the entire day. During the nights of ministry, there were miracles, signs, and wonders that happened. And people were so astonished.

On the last night of ministry, James called for everyone that needed prayer or something from God to come up, and he would pray for them. Then it was a man that came. His foot had been amputated, so he only had half his foot. And James stood there and asked the guy what he needed. He said, "I need for you to pray for my foot because ever since it was amputated, it has always been in pain."

James told the young man, "What I need for you to do is to go out and buy you a new pair of sneakers." And the gentleman replied, "Huh? I don't understand what you mean." James continued on to say, "If the store is closed today, tomorrow go out and buy you some sneakers." The gentleman asked him, "Why, Sir? There's nothing wrong with the tennis shoes I have on." James encouraged him, saying, "You need a new pair of sneakers because your foot is going to grow back. That's the reason why you're feeling pain". And his wife standing right next to him said, "Why would you tell my husband something like that and he just had his foot cut off? That doesn't make any sense." And then the young man said to James, "I had a dream that one day I woke up and my foot was there again. I, I didn't think anything of it, but I can't understand why you're telling me something like this." So, when the young man left, he went and bought the shoes.

When James came back the next night, the gentleman wasn't there. However, the Pastor had contacted James to tell him that the man had purchased the shoes as directed and would be back soon. Meanwhile, another Pastor came, and both Pastors invited James to speak across town. So, James ministered this time for five days straight. After speaking this time, he was really weary. James was exhausted and tired because he observed how the people who wanted something from God were the same people who kept coming back again, wanting something more. And he said to them, "Where is your faith? Is it that I must speak for something to happen to you? Is not the word of God enough for you?" And James became very disconcerted as he spoke each night. It seemed like the same people kept coming and kept coming but were never satisfied. They wanted the miracle but not the deliverance. The very thing that they needed, which was deliverance, they absolutely did not want. They didn't even bless God for the things that he had already given them.

And so, after this time, they wanted him to speak again, and James said, "I'm not speaking anymore. I'm tired." And he walked away from everyone.

No one knew where James had gone. He was tired and became even wearier. Finally, James started warring with the enemy. The warring was so overwhelming that James gave in? He said, "I'm not going to speak anymore because I'm tired. I'm tired of these people. They don't want to do right. And they keep asking for help. The only thing they need to do is just obey God and love him. They always want something from him, but they don't want to love him."

So, James didn't minister for months. However, something happened to James at that point. He started to get sick and he didn't know what was wrong with him. So, he went to the doctor and the doctor confirmed that there was something wrong, but he could not identify the problem. So, James talked with the doctor, and the doctor wanted to check him into the hospital to do some tests. James was in the hospital for almost two weeks while the doctors were running the tests. They were poking and sticking him every three hours. There were more and more tests. His blood pressure was fine. His sugar was fine, and all of his vitals were fine. They did so many MRI's and CAT scans. He was getting frustrated, and every time they wanted to send him home, something would happen. It pulled him back, and they made him stay in the hospital longer. James started getting very concerned. Finally, James said, "If there's nothing wrong, then I just need to check out of here." Then the doctor replied, "If we let you go, something serious can happen if we have missed anything." So, they had all types of specialists to come in over the next 2 ½ weeks.

While in the hospital one day, James noticed two men coming down the hallway. They went all the way to the end. They were going in to see many of the people that were sick. They had just come from church. The men said God told them to go and visit every person on that floor. One of the men was Apostle Benjamin. He went to every person on this floor. And once he came into James' room, he picked up his chart. The nurse said to him, "Sir, you need to put that down because that's confidential." And James said to him, "Don't worry about it. There's nothing on there anyway." The man said to James, "The Lord told me to ask you, are you tired of sitting here?" James said, "Yes, I am." And then he asked James, "Are you ready?" James answered, "Ready for what? Apostle Benjamin said to him, "You put your own self in this situation because you turned away from God. You told him what you were not going to do. Right now, you're living as the prophet did, in the mouth of a fish because you're rebelling against God. You told him you were not going to do it again." Then James broke down in tears. He said, "I'm just so tired of people just using him for what they want, not giving him any glory or anything. They say God understands you, and he hears you, but that's not your problem. You're here for purpose. You're here for His reason." And the Apostle said to James again, " My brother, are you ready?" And James said, "Yes, I'm ready." And he had some oil. The Apostle Benjamin said to James, "I'm getting ready to give you your Commission." Then put both of his hands on his own head, and he took his hands off his head, and he put both of his hands on James' head, and he spoke, "I point you and I strengthen you, and I Commission you in the name of Jesus Christ that who you are is an Apostle of Jesus Christ to speak his word. You have all the equipment that God has given you. Go forth and walk." And at that point, James got up like a storm. James got out of the bed. He signed himself out of the hospital and went home.

He had ten messages from people who wanted him to speak at their churches when James got home. So, he went back and began speaking from city to city. But this time, when he went, he spoke in many different churches with people of different nationalities. This one medium-sized church was a Methodist church. As he spoke there, the messages changed the people's lives, and they were converted. I know that might sound funny, but James didn't even think about it being

Methodist anymore because it wasn't a Methodist Church anymore after he was finished. Even the Pastor was converted. The congregants shouted and danced all over the church as their lives were changed.

Then all four pastors and the Methodist Pastor wanted James to minister, but they wanted him to minister in a place where everyone could hear him. So, they rented a Colosseum that could hold over 3000 people. James was concerned because, as he said before, he didn't like large crowds, but Apostle Benjamin told him, "Do not be concerned about the crowd. This is not about you. It's all about giving God glory and bringing his people back to him." So, when James came out, he prayed, and he fasted. He had been praying and fasting for three days. He didn't eat or drink? Then, James began to minister, and this time as James spoke, having his towel with him as always, he swung it at the crowd on the left side. The funny thing is that, when he swung it at the crowd, everyone from the bottom row on the floor all the way up to the top row fell out in the Spirit on the left-hand side.

Then James said, "If there is anyone in the building that cannot walk, I'm telling you to get up out of your chairs right now. Get up out of your wheelchairs right now. You don't need them. Get up right now." Suddenly, they all began getting up out of their wheelchairs after he spoke those words. They all got up out of their wheelchairs and began to praise God. For the first time in their life, they could walk. Remember the man that James told to purchase a new pair of shoes and that his foot would grow back in previous chapters came up. He was praising God for a while. This time the man was by himself. He wasn't with his wife anymore. When he came up, he said, "You see my sneakers? See my sneakers, see my sneakers." All the Pastors and Bishops and everyone was looking at him. James said, "I remember you. What happened?" The gentleman said, "Let me take my shoes off. Look at my feet. They're here. Both feet are here. My new one is a little bit longer than the other one, but I have both!"

As James moved on and the night grew to a close, he prayed for everyone in the Colosseum. James was very weary and tired because he had not prayed for that many people in one service before. So, he left the stage and changed his clothes. When he returned, he was sitting in a chair on the podium. The maintenance man came out and said, "I don't know how I'm going to get all this smoke out of here. I don't know what they sprayed in here or what they did, but this is like really odd smoke." The man continued, "I've never seen anything like this. When I turn the lights up brighter, it's not like it's cloudy. I can't even understand."

James asked the man, "You've never seen this smoke before, and the maintenance man responded," I've never seen anything like this." He also said," I've never seen the things that I've seen tonight. I was working the lights and I couldn't even believe all the things that I saw." James chuckled. Suddenly, the maintenance man said, "I know you're tired and everything, but can you do me this one favor?" James flipped over and he said, "What is that?" The maintenance man said, "I know I'm not worthy of this, but can you pray for me?" James said, "Sure." James commenced praying for him. As he prayed for him, the man fell out in the Spirit. James headed home, and he was really, really, tired. So when he arrived, he laid down and slept for three whole days, night and day. It didn't bother him one bit because he needed to rest.

Chapter 11
I Am

As the ministry went on, James prayed for people whenever they needed it. He went to the hospitals. He went to the streets. He preached in the tents. He continued to preach the word of God.

Looking back, James Jr. would remember the words of Jesus in John 3:16, "For God so loved the world that He gave his only begotten son, that whosoever shall believe in him shall not perish have everlasting life." When he would think about his life, the things that happened, the miracles God performed through him, John 14:12 would come to his mind, "Verily, verily I say unto you, he that believes in me, the works that I do, he shall do also. And greater works than these shall he do because I go unto my Father." Then James thought about how God had used him in so many different ways. God had changed his life forever.

One day James was going up to the hospital to visit a family member whose grandmother was on the verge of death because of old age. As James walked down the street en route to the hospital, he saw a sister attempted to comfort her brother. As soon James looked at them, he could see what was going on at that moment. The brother and his wife had just had a baby. The baby was born with a cord around her neck. His wife had started to hemorrhage while the medical team attempted to revive both the baby and his wife. As they were trying to revive them both, the brother held onto his sister and continued to cry. But as soon as James saw the man, he walked up to the young man and told him, "It's going to be alright. Go and see your wife and your little girl." The man looked at him and said, "Man, why would you say that? You don't even know me." James told him, "Trust me when I tell you. They that die, yet shall they live. Go and see your little girl and your wife. They're waiting on you." The man took off running.

James went on to pray with the family. When he prayed with the family, he talked to them about salvation. As James was getting ready to get into his car, the brother ran up to him, attempting to hug him. James was startled. The brother said, "I just want to thank you. They said they were gone. They were gone." The man was in shock. He went on to say, "How did you know? How did you know?" And James told him, "It's okay, go and be with your family." The brother asked James who he was. And James replied, "I am a friend." And James got in his car and drove away. The guy just stared in James' direction as he drove off. I'm saying this to you because there are so many who don't believe. The Bible says to us in Matthew 6:33, "Seek ye first the kingdom of God and his righteousness and all these things will be added unto you." Yet, we limit God so much.

I want to tell you something about the man James you have read of in this book. James and I are one and the same. I am James. I am Apostle Clarence, and this is my story. My purpose for writing this book is to help people get rid of their limiting beliefs. We limit God in so many things. There are so many times we ask God for something, and then we go and try to fix it for ourselves. We never give God the time to do what He said He would do because of our lack of faith. Jesus said these things would come to those who believe. The only thing that we have to do is believe, and nothing is impossible. I tell you today, Jesus is soon to come, Jesus is soon to come. Ask yourself the question, "Are you ready for him?" He is ready for us, but are you ready for him? Have you made yourself ready for him?

Revelations 3:20 says, "Behold I stand at the door and knock, if any man hears my voice and opens the door, I will come into him and I will sup with him and he with me." A part of believing is accepting Him as your Lord and savior. Romans 10:9-10 says, "If thou shalt confess with thy mouth the Lord Jesus and shall believe in thou heart that God has raised Him from the dead, thou shall be saved. For with the heart man believe unto righteousness and with the mouth confession is made unto salvation."

There are so many people that profess with their mouths, but they don't believe with their hearts because they're still holding on to the old baggage, that old unforgiveness, that person that hurt them in their life. We don't understand that if we can't forgive those people and leave them at the cross (because Jesus died on the cross for us), then how can we expect God to forgive us? We have to learn to forgive because to believe in your heart means that you're opening up your heart. That means you're opening up the door for Him to come in and sit with you and clean out all that old baggage, all that old dirt, all the old problems, and everything that's ever happened in your life. I truly hope that you will start believing today because he said you would do greater works. You may think that you have to have a title to do this work. Titles do not matter. No! The appointment comes with those who believe! God bless you.

About The Author
Apostle Clarence Kittrell

Author - Apostle Clarence Kittrell is one of God's Anointed Men of Faith and Power. God has used Kittrell to bring salvation, healing, and deliverance from sickness and demonic spirits to thousands. God has worked many miracles through this humble servant throughout the United States and in many foreign countries.

He is an Apostle to the nations who has devoted his life to preaching the Good News of Jesus Christ and walking in his footsteps.

He served in the US Army for four years and was awarded two bronze stars for bravery. He currently holds a Bachelor's Degree in Marketing from Methodist University. Additionally, he holds three certificates; Pastoral Studies, Biblical Teaching, and

Divinity from Oral Roberts University.

Apostle Kittrell is a devoted husband and father who truly understands what the titles, husband and father mean. He has acquired many followers through "True Vine Church of Faith and Deliverance" and "True Vine Love Ministries International." Apostle Clarence has had a unique love for God's people and a burden to win souls at all costs and since 1990. He strongly sets the example that encourages all races to recognize that color shouldn't matter; we all belong to Jesus Christ.

Apostle Clarence has been given an Apostolic-Prophetic message of divine order by God to impact the world! This message, framed with healing and deliverance for the 21st-century church, comes powerfully packaged in his sermons, teachings, and most recently through his literary works. His most current written work, *Denied Love*, is a heartwarming chronicle of extraordinary events from the life of an ordinary man. This heartwarming account will leave you scratching your head, wanting for more, and sometimes even having that proverbial Deja-vu moment. *Denied Love* is a confirming word of how the power and love of God are undeniably available to all of us.

He is currently working on the next series of books, *A Shattered Heart Reaching Through A Broken Window, God Deals In Specifics, Where Is Adam?* and *Understanding The Love of Jesus Christ.*

www.ingramcontent.com/pod-product-compliance
Lightning Source LLC
Chambersburg PA
CBHW011318080526
44589CB00020B/2747